P9-BZU-545

DATE DUE

AUG 3 1 1989			
SEP 1 4 1989			
SEP 2 8 1989			

DEMCO 38-297

Buffalo Hunt

Buffalo Hunter. Artist unknown, circa 1844.

COLLECTION OF THE SANTA BARBARA MUSEUM OF ART, GIFT OF HARRIETT COWLES HAMMETT GRAHAM IN MEMORY OF BUELL HAMMETT.

Buffalo Hunt

Russell Freedman

Holiday House / New York

For Thomas Cuyler Stedman Perkins

"Goodnight, Moon!"

Cheyenne pipe bowl, black stone.   DENVER ART MUSEUM.

Copyright © 1988 by Russell Freedman
All rights reserved
Printed in the United States of America
First Edition

Library of Congress Cataloging-in-Publication Data

Freedman, Russell.
Buffalo hunt/written by Russell Freedman.— 1st ed.
p. cm.
Includes index.
Summary: Examines the importance of the buffalo in the lore and
day-to-day life of the Indian tribes of the Great Plains and
describes hunting methods and the uses found for each part of the
animal that could not be eaten.
ISBN 0-8234-0702-0
1. Indians of North America—Great Plains—Juvenile literature.
2. Indians of North America—Great Plains—Hunting—Juvenile
literature. 3: Bison, American—Juvenile literature. [1. Indians
of North America—Great Plains. 2. Indians of North America—Great
Plains—Hunting. 3. Bison.] I. Title.
E78.G73F73 1988
978′ .00497—dc19 87-35303 CIP AC

978
F

Contents

140759

NATIONAL MUSEUM OF AMERICAN ART, SMITHSONIAN INSTITUTION.

Buffalo Bull Grazing on the Prairie. George Catlin.
Between 1830 and 1836 Catlin traveled through unmapped
Indian country and made more than 500 dramatic paintings.

6

A Gift from the Great Spirit

Over blazing campfires on winter nights, Indian storytellers spoke of the buffalo. They told tales of buffalo giants and buffalo ghosts, of buffalo that changed magically into men, of children who were raised by buffalo and understood their language.

In olden times, it was said, buffalo used to eat Indians. They ate so many Indians that a legendary figure called Old Man had to put a stop to it. He organized a race between the buffalo and the Indians to decide who should eat whom. The Indians won.

On the Great Plains of North America, every Indian tribe had a rich and ready store of buffalo tales and legends. According to the Comanche, buffalo came from gigantic caves somewhere on the windswept ranges of the Texas Panhandle. Each spring, the Great Spirit sent throngs of buffalo from those hidden caves onto the open plains, as a gift to the Indian people.

Up North, the Blackfoot said that a lake in Canada was the place where the buffalo began. They were born beneath the water, in the darkest depths of the lake. If you could visit that sacred spot on the right night, at exactly the right time, you would hear an eerie rumbling coming from the middle of the lake. Then you would see the buffalo rise out of the water and crowd onto the shore, their shaggy fur wet and dripping, their curved horns gleaming in the moonlight.

To the Plains Indians, the buffalo, or American bison, was the most important animal on earth. This snorting, lumbering beast provided almost everything the Indians needed to stay alive. The buffalo kept their bellies full and their bodies warm. It supplied raw materials for their weapons, tools, ornaments, and toys. The rhythm of their daily lives was ruled by the comings and goings of the great buffalo herds.

It is little wonder that the Indians worshiped the buffalo as a sacred animal. Before and after every hunt, they praised the spirit of the buffalo and thanked him for giving his meat. Men, women, and children carried buffalo-shaped rocks and fossils for good luck. They believed in the powerful magic of buffalo dreams. When they died, they hoped to go to a happy hunting ground in the sky where buffalo flourished. Looking into the night sky, the Pawnee believed that the Milky Way was formed by dust left behind by the spirit-buffalo.

As recently as 150 years ago, countless millions of buffalo still roamed the prairies and plains. They ranged from the Mississippi River westward to the Rockies, and from Canada down to the Rio

Grande. Native American hunters had been stalking the animals for many thousands of years. During most of that time, the Indians had neither horses nor guns. They hunted on foot, and they killed their prey with stone-tipped arrows and spears. They knew how to creep up on a grazing herd, how to surround the buffalo, and how to drive them into corrals or stampede them over cliffs.

Without horses, the Indians had to travel on foot whenever they moved their encampments. Back then, they used big shaggy dogs as pack animals to help carry their tipis and other belongings. Sometimes on a long journey the dogs would grow tired and begin to droop and lag and hang their tongues. Then someone would cry, "Buffalo ahead! Fresh meat in plenty!" And the dogs would bound forward as though they had just set out. Later, the Indians would remember that era as their Dog Days.

The first horses were brought to North America by Spanish explorers in the 1500s. Within a century or so, runaway horses had drifted northward from Spanish settlements in Mexico and were roaming the plains in wild herds. The Indians learned to capture and tame those wild horses, and the horses changed their lives.

Now they could travel long distances to find the buffalo. They could chase the herds and kill the choicest animals. And with packhorses, they could carry bigger tipis and more possessions with them as they traveled across the plains. In time, the Indians became some of the world's finest horsemen, experts at hunting and fighting on horseback.

When white trappers and traders began to visit the Great Plains in the early 1800s, about 250,000 Indians were living in the region. They belonged to some two dozen distinct tribes, each with its own language and customs. Many of these tribes had migrated from the woodlands of the East, but only a few, like the Pawnee of Kansas and Nebraska, still practiced the old arts of farming and fishing.

Most of the Plains Indians had given up the settled life of farmers and fishermen to follow the buffalo herds. They spent the winter in sheltered camps. But in spring they folded their tipis and roamed the plains. They hunted other animals beside the buffalo, of course —deer, antelope, elk, and an occasional bear. But buffalo meat was their staple food, buffalo hunting their main occupation.

A plains tribe was made up of many small, independent bands. Once or twice a year, all the bands belonging to a tribe would assemble for a great religious ceremony, a tribal council, or a communal hunt. But mostly, the bands moved about on their own. Each band had its own encampments, or villages. And each band hunted in a different part of the tribal territory.

Hunting was a man's responsibility. Every able-bodied boy was taught that he should become a fearless hunter and warrior. Small boys ran about yip-yapping in play hunts, dreaming of the day when they would be big enough to ride after a herd of stampeding buffalo. A successful hunter could provide for many people. He became a man of influence, entitled to honors and privileges.

Women were responsible for putting the buffalo and other game to good use. It was a woman's job to skin and butcher the buffalo, to

Catching the Wild Horse. George Catlin.

THE THOMAS GILCREASE INSTITUTE OF AMERICAN HISTORY
AND ART, TULSA, OKLAHOMA.

preserve the meat and tan the hides. As Indian girls grew up, they learned from their mothers and grandmothers the art of transforming a dead buffalo into a thousand practical and useful objects.

The buffalo was the biggest animal on the plains. A full-grown bull stood six feet tall at the humped shoulders and weighed a ton or more. An angry bull could stab a bear to death. He could toss a wolf so high into the air that the wolf would be killed by the fall.

While buffalo were somewhat dim-sighted, they could hear the faintest sounds and smell enemies from three miles away. And when they sensed danger, they moved fast. A bull or cow could wheel about on its slim hind legs and run as fast as a horse. When a whole herd stampeded, the earth trembled.

Comanche Feats of Horsemanship. George Catlin.

THE NEW YORK HISTORICAL SOCIETY.

JOSLYN ART MUSEUM, OMAHA, NEBRASKA.

Assiniboin Camp. Karl Bodmer. Bodmer visited this encampment of
Assiniboin Indians on June 30, 1833. The tipi in the foreground,
the dwelling of a chief, has large bear figures painted on its sides.

Buffalo and Elk on the Upper Missouri. Karl Bodmer.

JOSLYN ART MUSEUM, OMAHA, NEBRASKA.

White explorers were astonished at the size of the herds they saw as they crossed the Great Plains. There were times when buffalo stretched endlessly across the countryside as far as the eye could see. Artist George Catlin described these herds when he traveled west during the 1830s to study and paint the Indians. "Buffalo graze in immense herds and almost incredible numbers," he wrote. "And they roam over vast tracts of country."

No one really knows how many buffalo roamed the prairies and plains before the white man came. The Indians thought there were enough buffalo to last forever. It seemed impossible that they could ever disappear.

Leader of the Mandan Buffalo Bull Society. Karl Bodmer.
Only the bravest Mandan warriors were permitted to
wear the complete buffalo-head mask shown here.
The decorations on the shield are symbols of this
warrior's personal medicine, or power.

Buffalo Magic

The best time for hunting came in late
summer or early fall, when the grass was
tall and the buffalo were putting on their
winter fat.

All across the plains, hunting bands
prepared to break camp and follow the
grazing herds. The Indians would hunt
until they had enough meat and hides to
last the winter—or until the first deep
snows.

A big hunt was always a community af-
fair. Every man, woman, and child went
along and took part. As the time

approached, people talked about little else but the coming event.

It was the job of the shaman, or medicine man, to attract the buffalo within easy reach, or guide the hunters to the nearest herd. For this he needed the aid and cooperation of the spirits. Without their help, the buffalo would stay out of range, and the hunters would lack courage and skill.

A medicine man was not simply a doctor, or healer. People honored him as a spiritual leader, a holy man, a prophet with mysterious powers. He was expected to cure sickness, cast spells, and see into the future. He learned his secrets from the host of spirits that existed everywhere—in the sky, on earth, and in all living creatures.

"The spirits talk to me," said a famous Sioux shaman. "I can give magic power to things."

Before a hunt, the medicine man sought dreams and visions that would reveal where the buffalo gathered. He offered prayers, sang songs, and performed rituals to win the favor of the spirits and make the hunt a success.

Often he prayed to a buffalo skull, which was considered sacred. After a buffalo had been killed, its spirit was believed to stay in or about the skull until the horns dropped off and were swallowed by the earth. The medicine man's prayer was meant to summon the buffalo's spirit.

The Sioux would paint a buffalo skull red. They decorated it with feathers and fancy quillwork and attached small medicine bundles —collections of holy objects prepared by a medicine man. Then the skull was placed in the center of the council lodge, the tipi where the tribal council met.

The Northern Cheyenne felt there was powerful medicine in their sacred buffalo hat. It was made from the hide of a buffalo cow's head, with two hand-painted horns attached. The hat was kept in a place of honor along with four stone-headed medicine arrows, two for war and two for hunting. When a Cheyenne warrior took an oath, he would swear by the medicine arrows and the buffalo hat— just as we swear by the Bible.

Assiniboin Medicine Sign. Karl Bodmer. A buffalo skull mounted on a rock was a medicine sign—a magical device intended to attract buffalo herds to Assiniboin lands.

JOSLYN ART MUSEUM, OMAHA, NEBRASKA.

Buffalo Dance of the Mandan Indians. George Catlin.

Buffalo masks and headdresses were a familiar part of the ceremonial dances held before every hunt. Indian dancers imitated the movements of the buffalo—pawing, milling, stampeding—in hopes of encouraging a herd to approach. By the light of a campfire or an autumn moon, dancers, singers, and drummers lifted their voices and stamped their feet late into the night. Sometimes the dance went on for days without stopping, as different performers stepped in to take their turns.

In 1832, George Catlin watched the buffalo dance of the Mandan Indians, who lived on the upper reaches of the Missouri River in present-day North Dakota. The dance took place in the center of the village, in front of the great medicine or mystery lodge, where the most treasured religious objects were kept. Between ten and fifteen Mandan at a time joined in the dance. Their bodies were painted with black, white, or red stripes. Each dancer wore a horned buffalo-hair mask. In his hand he held his favorite spear or bow.

"Drums are beating and rattles are shaken," wrote Catlin, "and songs and yells incessantly are shouted, and lookers-on stand ready with masks on their heads, and weapons in hand, to take the place of each dancer as he becomes fatigued and jumps out of the ring."

Mandan women, belonging to the White Buffalo Cow Society, performed their own dance to lure the buffalo. They wore tall headdresses made from the skin of a sacred white buffalo and decorated with feathers. Wrapped in colorful robes, they danced in position, raising each foot in turn and swaying from side to side.

A hunt was planned and organized by all the leaders of a band, meeting around their council fire. They would discuss the hunt among themselves and agree on a plan, deciding when to begin and which part of the tribal territory to select for hunting. Then they would choose several young warriors of good character to serve as marshals, or police. Appointment as a hunt marshal was a great honor, a big step toward becoming a leader.

Among the Sioux, each marshal was presented with a scalp shirt and a feathered banner as symbols of his authority. He would then dip his finger in black paint and draw a stripe down his right cheek, from his eye to his chin. This was his badge of office.

During a hunt, the marshals and their assistants were in charge of the camp and everyone in it. It was their duty to enforce the rules and regulations of the hunt. Those rules were strict. They were recognized by all: Everyone must stay together. No one was allowed to go after the buffalo by himself. Anyone who startled or stampeded the herd must be punished. The marshals alone must direct the approach to the herd and the attack on the buffalo. The meat from a hunt must be fairly and equally divided among all members of the hunting party.

Since the band's survival depended on a successful hunt, anyone who broke the rules would be punished by the marshals. Punish-

Dance of the Mandan Women. Aquatint by Ch. Geoffroy after Bodmer.

LIBRARY OF CONGRESS.

MUSEUM OF THE AMERICAN INDIAN, HEYE FOUNDATION.

Traditional Indian artists developed a unique style of their own. This painted elkskin robe, the work of a Crow artist, depicts a Buffalo hunt.

ments ranged from a warning to a fine to a whipping. The marshals had the power to take away an offender's property, destroy his tipi, or kill his horse. They could bar him from taking part in the hunt, or in any of the band's activities.

Before setting out, the hunters took great care to groom their horses and prepare their weapons. When a warrior rode off to meet the buffalo, he tucked a knife in his belt and carried either a spear or a bow with a quiver of arrows. The bow was a short one, no more than three feet, that could be handled easily on horseback. It might be made of ash or hickory wood, or of elk or mountain-sheep horn. Often it was reinforced with twisted sinews of buffalo or deer, and it was usually carved, painted, or ornamented. Crow and Blackfoot warriors covered their bows with rattlesnake skins. It took as long as three months to make a fine bow.

Buffalo Chase with Bows and Lances. George Catlin. If a rider fell, he could grab the rawhide strap trailing on the ground behind his horse.

Arrows were about two feet long and might be made of dogwood or cane. They were tipped with stone, bone, or horn, or in later times, with metal points. And they were carried in a quiver made of panther or otter skin.

Most Indian hunters continued to use spears and bows even after the white man had introduced firearms to the plains. The old-fashioned muskets of the time were difficult to load on horseback. A skilled warrior could shoot a stream of arrows faster than a man

NATIONAL MUSEUM OF AMERICAN ART, SMITHSONIAN INSTITUTION.

armed with a musket could reload and fire. It wasn't until repeating rifles were introduced in the 1870s that Indians began to discard their bows and arrows.

A hunter's most prized possession was his horse. A trained hunting horse had to be strong enough to gallop long distances, fast enough to overtake a stampeding herd, and calm enough to dash into the midst of the herd, dodging the buffalo's horns. Such a horse was used only for hunting, in war parties, or for racing. It was never put to work as a packhorse.

The hunter usually rode bareback, stripped down to his breechcloth and moccasins, with his quiver of about twenty arrows strapped to his back. Fastened to his horse's neck was a long rawhide strap, which trailed behind the horse on the ground. If the rider fell, he could grab the trailing strap, slow the horse with his dragging body, pull himself to his feet, and leap back on his horse.

A Buffalo Hunt on the Southwestern Prairies. John Mix Stanley, 1845.

NATIONAL MUSEUM OF AMERICAN ART, SMITHSONIAN INSTITUTION.

The Hunt

On the day set for starting a hunt, everyone was up at sunrise. The women went right to work, packing their household belongings and getting everything ready for the move. Youngsters rounded up the horses and dogs. The men gathered in small groups to discuss the day's plans.

After a quick morning meal, the marshals assembled. They took their feathered banners in their hands, mounted their horses, and gave the signal to break camp.

With that, the Indian village disappeared almost like a puff of smoke. Tipis dropped to the ground as the women removed the buffalo-skin walls and took down the long poles that held the tipis erect.

The poles were now put to a different use. Lashed to the sides of

Band of Sioux Moving Camp with Dogs and Horses. George Catlin.

a horse so they trailed behind on the ground, the poles supported a sturdy rawhide platform called a travois (tra-VOY). This platform held the folded tipi walls and the family's household goods. Sometimes small children or sick people sat on top of the pile to be hauled along by a strong packhorse. Dogs also worked as pack animals, pulling travois designed to fit their size and strength.

When the horses and dogs were harnessed and loaded and ready to go, the people and their animals moved out across the plains. The warriors, mounted on the best hunting horses, rode along in front. They were followed by boys and girls driving the herd of extra horses. Behind them came the women leading the packhorses, along with the small children and the old folks, some riding, some walking, and some being carried on the travois. Every woman had a heavy pack on her back. The men never carried packs. They kept their arms free to use their weapons in case of a surprise attack.

Scouts rode far ahead of the marching people, and far to either side, watching for signs of buffalo or lurking enemies. Other warriors acted as a rear guard. They followed the group at a distance, seeing that no one lagged behind.

Strung out across the prairie, the Indians formed a grand procession. People sang as they marched along, dogs barked, horses whinnied, bells jingled. They moved forward each day by easy stages, so their horses would be in good condition when they found the buffalo.

At the end of a day's march, the marshals picked the spot where they would pitch camp. The women quickly put up the tipis and prepared the evening meal as the men gathered to chat and smoke. On the open plains, the Indians usually camped in a circle, with the doorway of each tipi facing east to catch the morning sun.

NATIONAL MUSEUM OF AMERICAN ART, SMITHSONIAN INSTITUTION.

Crow Lodge of Twenty-five Buffalo Skins. George Catlin.

When they reached the territory where they expected to hunt, the scouts fanned out across the countryside, looking for buffalo. Everyone else waited in the hushed camp. Marshals moved quietly from one tipi to the next. They reminded people in low tones not to sing or shout or make any loud noise that might scare off the buffalo, which could hear weak and distant sounds.

The scouts, meanwhile, searched for buffalo signs. Sometimes they relied on animal helpers. The Comanche watched for ravens. They thought that if a raven circled four times overhead and cawed, it would then fly off toward the buffalo. A Cheyenne hunter would find a cricket, hold it in his hand, and wait to see which way its antennae pointed. The buffalo, he believed, would be found in that direction.

When a herd was sighted, the successful scout rushed back to camp. As he arrived, people crowded around, greeting him with congratulations and thanks. First he smoked a ceremonial pipe with one of the band's elders. Then he reported what he had seen.

The chase usually started the next morning. As soon as it was light enough to see, the hunters mounted their horses. Riding close together, they stayed downwind from the herd, so the buffalo would not catch their scent.

When they were as close as they could get without disturbing the buffalo, they paused and waited. The marshals looked over the area and selected the best spot to launch the attack. Silently, they led the hunters forward and spaced them evenly, so that each would have a fair start. Then one of the marshals rode out in view of both

The Buffalo Hunt No. 39. Charles M. Russell, 1919. Russell painted the buffalo hunt many times. In this scene, the hunters are using arrows, lances, and firearms.

hunters and buffalo. He waved his hand above his head, and the chase began.

Bending low over their horses, the Indians galloped toward the grazing herd. At first the buffalo paid little attention. Often the hunters would almost reach the herd before the buffalo became alarmed and started to run.

Each man acted on his own now. Holding his bow in his left hand, urging his horse on with the whip strapped to his right wrist, a hunter picked his target and went after it at full speed. His horse was trained to approach the buffalo from the right, so the rider could shoot his arrow to the left, toward the animal. As he closed in,

AMON CARTER MUSEUM, FORT WORTH.

29

he aimed for a spot just behind the buffalo's last rib, where the arrow would pierce the animal's lungs. A single well-aimed arrow could kill the biggest buffalo.

Sometimes an arrow would strike with such force that it would be completely buried. It might pass all the way through the animal, come out the other side, and drop to the ground. If an arrow failed to go deep enough, the hunter might reach over, pull it out of the buffalo, and use it again.

Once an arrow hit its mark, the hunter instantly took off after another buffalo. His horse understood exactly what to do. Running free, guided only by words or knee pressure, a trained hunting pony would leap away from a buffalo's horns as soon as it heard the twang of the bowstring.

Some men found the bow and arrow too tame. They preferred to use spears, for it took more strength and courage to spear a buffalo. To carry only a spear on the hunt was a mark of daring and pride.

With any weapon, the chase was risky. Horses stumbled in prairie-dog holes. Wounded buffalo lashed out with their horns. Sometimes an enraged bull crashed headlong into a horse and rider. The buffalo claimed many victims as hunters were trampled in the dust or died of broken bones.

While the chase was thrilling, it wasn't always the best way to hunt. During a typical chase on horseback, each hunter might bring down two or three buffalo. Under the right conditions, the Indians could get better results with less danger by hunting in the old way—on foot.

In that case, they would stake their horses and creep up on the buffalo, crawling on hands and knees through tall grass. As long as

Buffalo Hunt under the Wolfskin Mask. George Catlin. Because healthy buffalo did not fear wolves, hunters disguised in wolfskins could crawl to the edge of a herd before shooting their arrows.

the Indians were hidden, the buffalo would go right on grazing, even as arrows flew silently around them. Each man might shoot several buffalo in quick succession before the others became frightened and ran off.

In winter, when the grass offered little cover, a hunter might sneak up on a herd disguised in a buffalo robe. Or he could drape himself in the skin of a white wolf. Healthy buffalo in herds did not fear wolves and didn't run when they saw one.

NATIONAL MUSEUM OF AMERICAN ART, SMITHSONIAN INSTITUTION,

If a herd was small enough, the Indians sometimes surrounded the buffalo on foot. Approaching downwind, they fanned out, moved in from all sides, and formed a tight ring. Then they ran in circles around the herd, whooping and yelling and waving their arms as the terrified animals milled about in confusion. Slowly the Indians closed the circle until they were close enough to let go with their arrows and spears.

The first buffalo to be hit would fall near the outside of the circle, blocking the path of those inside the ring. As more buffalo fell, their bodies trapped the others. Sometimes not a single animal escaped alive.

On horseback, the Indians could surround bigger herds, galloping around them in a circle. One afternoon in 1832, George Catlin, armed with his pencil and sketchbook, watched from a distance as 500 Sioux horsemen surrounded a herd near the present site of Pierre, South Dakota. By sundown, the hunters had killed 1,400 buffalo.

The Indians knew the instincts and habits of the buffalo. They knew how to coax a herd in any direction by gently spooking the animals. Hunters would show themselves along the flanks of the herd and slowly walk forward. The herd moved forward too, since buffalo will always try to pass in front of any enemy flanking them. Flankers on each side of a herd, and chasers in the rear, could nudge the animals into a swamp, a lake, or a river, and kill them there.

When snow covered the plains, hunters on rawhide snowshoes

Buffalo Chase in Winter, Indians on Snowshoes. George Catlin.

NATIONAL MUSEUM OF AMERICAN ART, SMITHSONIAN INSTITUTION.

would herd buffalo into deep drifts or ravines. As the animals floundered about, the Indians could kill them easily with spears, arrows, or guns.

Some tribes built corrals of timber or stone, designed to trap elk, deer, and wild horses, as well as buffalo. Extending from the narrow entrance to the corral were two long fences, which spread out across the countryside like a pair of wings. Where timber or stone was scarce, the wing fences might be built of piled brush or buffalo bones.

When buffalo came into the area, they were lured between the fences and then driven toward the corral entrance. Sometimes a hunter dressed in buffalo robes walked ahead of the herd, bleating like a calf, leading the animals on. As the buffalo approached the corral, more hunters came out of hiding to join those who were driving the animals. Once they were trapped inside the corral walls, the buffalo could be killed with little risk.

In some regions, hunters could stampede the animals over the edge of a high cliff. Hidden by tall grass, they would creep up behind a herd. Then they would jump to their feet, shrieking and waving robes, taking the buffalo by surprise.

The startled herd would take off, galloping away from the Indians and heading toward the cliff. As the buffalo in the lead approached the edge of the cliff, they tried to veer away at the last minute. But it was too late. Other stampeding buffalo plowed into the leaders from behind, and they all went tumbling over.

On the ground below, Indians were waiting with spears to finish off any injured animals that survived the fall. After that, the women moved in to start the butchering.

Hunting Buffalo. Alfred Jacob Miller, circa 1858.

WALTERS ART GALLERY, BALTIMORE.

From the Brains to the Tail

Before the skinning and butchering began, a medicine man chose one of the dead animals as a religious offering.

If a white buffalo had died, it was chosen. Its skin was removed, to be saved as a rare and sacred object. The rest of the carcass was left untouched where it had fallen. The spirit of the buffalo would find a resting place there, and be pleased with the generosity of the hunters.

By now, the women, children, and old people had come to the scene of the hunt with packhorses and travois to carry away the meat and hides. Each wife picked out the animals her warrior had killed, recognizing them by the special markings on his arrows. If a hunter had used too many arrows to kill one buffalo, the women would laugh and make fun of him.

As a rule the hide belonged to the hunter who had killed the animal. It was claimed by the women in his household. The meat taken during a hunt was divided equally among all the members of the band. Extra meat and hides were set aside for the aged, the ailing, and for orphans.

Skinning and butchering were mainly jobs for the women and older girls. The men moved the animals into position. Then the women took their sharp flint knives, slashed open the hides, and

Dying Buffalo. George Catlin.

NATIONAL MUSEUM OF AMERICAN ART, SMITHSONIAN INSTITUTION.

peeled them back. After a hide was removed, they butchered the meat. It was cut into pieces that could be bagged in buffalo skins and carried to camp.

Parts of the buffalo that spoiled quickly were eaten on the spot. As the women worked, the hunters devoured thin slices of raw liver, still warm and smoking, dipped in the salty juices of gallbladders. They ate mouthfuls of raw brains, taken from the cracked skulls. Sometimes they built fires right there on the hunting grounds and barbecued the small intestines.

When the butchering was finished, the hides and meat were loaded on the packhorses. As the Indians headed back to camp, they might leave hundreds of buffalo hearts behind them, strewn across the plain. They believed that the magical power of those hearts would help renew the herd.

A successful hunt called for a feast. Beside the campfire that evening, a medicine man offered prayers of thanksgiving. He thanked the spirits for their aid during the chase, and he thanked the buffalo for giving his meat to the people. Choice bits of meat were sliced off, held up for the spirits to see, then buried as an offering.

There was plenty for everyone to eat. A single fat buffalo cow supplied enough meat to feed a hundred hungry people. They gorged themselves on fresh tongue roasted over the open fire, on tasty morsels cut from the buffalo's hump. They ate hot, dripping ribs and steaks. And they feasted on yards of roasted gut, turned inside out, stuffed with chunks of meat, and seared over glowing coals. The sweet, nutritious bone marrow was saved for the old folks. It was the only meat their toothless gums could chew.

Most of the meat taken during a big hunt was preserved for the future. The women cut the meat into strips and hung it over high poles to dry. After several days, this sun-dried meat, called jerky, was so well preserved that it would last for months. It could be carried anywhere and would not spoil, even during the hottest months.

Some of the dried meat was pounded to a pulp, mixed with buffalo fat, and flavored with crushed nuts, berries, and fruit. This was called pemmican. Packed in buffalo-skin bags, pemmican would last for years without spoiling. Sliced and dipped in wild honey, it was nourishing and delicious, a favorite food among the Indians, and later the white fur traders as well.

Every part of the buffalo that could be chewed, swallowed, and digested was used for food. And every other part was put to some use.

Indian women spent a great deal of time and effort tanning buffalo hides. After a hunt, the fresh hides were spread out on the ground, hairy side down, and pegged in place. Using scrapers made of buffalo bone, the women scraped all the flesh, fat, and blood from the hides. They cured and bleached the hides in the sun, and soaked them in a tanning fluid of buffalo brains, liver, and fat mixed with water. Then they worked the hides for several days— rubbing, kneading, squeezing, stretching—to make them soft and supple. A good hunter might have several wives working on hides taken from the animals he had killed.

If the hides were to be used as winter robes, the hair was left in place. Thick-furred buffalo robes made warm and comfortable cloaks and bedding. They could be cut and stitched into caps, ear-

AMON CARTER MUSEUM, FORT WORTH.

The Silk Robe. Charles M. Russell, circa 1890. Two women prepare a buffalo skin for tanning. An especially fine buffalo robe required ten days of steady labor. It was called a "silk robe" because of the softness of the leather and the sheen of the fur.

muffs, leggings, and mittens. The finest robes came from buffalo killed during the winter, when nature gave the animal a full coat to protect it from snow and cold.

With the hair scraped off, the hides were smoked over fires to make them waterproof. They could then be fashioned into dozens of useful articles. They were used for the walls of tipis, for clothing and moccasins, for pouches, purses, and saddlebags. Babies were carried in cradleboards lined with the softest buffalo calfskin. The dead were laid to rest wrapped in buffalo-hide winding sheets.

Thick rawhide from the necks of old bulls was stretched to make tough war shields and the soles of winter moccasins. Strong sinews from the neck and back of the buffalo provided bowstrings and

Biróhkä, a Hidatsa Man. Karl Bodmer. Biróhkä is wearing a beautifully painted buffalo robe. His hat, made from the hide of a white buffalo, shows that he is a man of substance.

JOSLYN ART MUSEUM, OMAHA, NEBRASKA.

41

thread. The buffalo's hair was twisted into ropes and bridles, woven into ornaments, stuffed into leather balls. Its stomach became a water jug, its tail a flyswatter.

Buffalo horns were used for cups, ladles, and spoons, and to carry hot coals to the next campground. The hooves produced glue; the fat, soap. The bones were shaped into knives, spears, and tools of many kinds. On the northern plains, the backbone with ribs attached made a toboggan for children in winter.

Even the buffalo's droppings were valuable. On the treeless plains, firewood was scarce. But there was an endless supply of sun-dried buffalo dung left behind by the grazing herds. These prized "buffalo chips" burned slowly, produced a hot fire, and were ideal for cooking. They were used for that purpose by the Indians, and later by white settlers too.

A fall buffalo hunt would continue until the band had all the hides and meat it needed for the winter. Then the Indians would settle down in their winter camps. Every band had its favorite winter camping sites near woods, in a sheltered canyon, or along a river bottom. Instead of camping in a circle, as they did on the open plains, the Indians pitched their winter tipis in a line that sometimes stretched for miles along the canyon floor or the river's banks.

A tipi provided a warm and cozy winter home. Because it was shaped like a cone, it could withstand the most violent winds and blizzards. Its walls were waterproof. An open fire in the center of the tipi furnished heat, light, and a stove for indoor cooking. The smoke spiraled up through an adjustable smoke hole at the top of the tipi. At night, firelight would shine through the translucent

Comanche Village in Texas, Women Dressing Robes and Drying Meat. George Catlin.

NATIONAL MUSEUM OF AMERICAN ART, SMITHSONIAN INSTITUTION.

buffalo-skin walls, and from the outside, the tipi glowed like a lantern.

Tipis were usually owned by the women who made them. A typical tipi measured perhaps fifteen feet across at the base, allowing sufficient living space for the family and its possessions. It could be put up in fifteen minutes by the women of the household. It could be taken down in five minutes. And it could be packed on a horse travois and carried anywhere.

When the hunting was good, the Indians went into winter camp with tons of sun-dried buffalo meat. They didn't have to hunt day after day, all winter long, for fear of starving. Between hunts, they were free to do as they wished. "It was a great life," said Tom Le Forge, a white man who lived several years with the Crows. "At all times I had ample leisure for lazy loafing and dreaming and visiting."

With the Buffalo Gone

Year after year without fail, the buffalo drifted back and forth across the plains in tune with the seasons. Usually they traveled in small bands. But during the late summer rutting season, they gathered in enormous herds that numbered hundreds of thousands of animals. A truly great herd might be fifty miles long and take days to pass by.

Indians had hunted the buffalo for thousands of years without making much of a dent in the herds. Sometimes they killed more animals than they could use. When they drove a herd over a cliff, they could not always carry away all the meat. But for the most part, the Indians were not wasteful. They hunted only when they needed meat and hides.

As white people came to the plains, the buffalo herds began to dwindle. By the early 1800s, trading posts were springing up all over the West. White traders wanted buffalo robes and tongues for profitable markets in the East. In exchange, they offered guns, tools, tobacco, whiskey, and trinkets. The Indians had always hunted for their own needs. Now, by killing a few more buffalo, they could obtain the white man's goods.

Soon the Indians were killing buffalo for their hides and tongues alone. Tongues packed in salt were shipped in barges down the Missouri River, to be sent to the cities of the East, where they were sold as an expensive delicacy. Buffalo robes became fashionable as lap robes and blankets. White people had them made into fur coats. During the 1830s and 1840s, hundreds of thousands of robes were shipped east.

BUFFALO BILL HISTORICAL CENTER, CODY, WYOMING.

Last of the Buffalo. Albert Bierstadt, 1888. With this painting, Bierstadt said that he wanted to "depict the cruel slaughter of a noble animal now almost extinct."

By then, white hunters were beginning to kill more buffalo than the Indians. Pioneers traveling westward in covered wagons shot the animals for food along the way, scaring off entire herds. Before long, few buffalo could be found along the great trails leading west. Then the United States Army hired professional hunters to supply buffalo meat to western military posts. And as railroads were built across the prairies and plains, white hunters furnished buffalo meat for the railroad construction crews.

Buffalo hunting became a popular sport. Many travelers felt that a trip west wasn't complete unless they had shot themselves a buffalo. American millionaires and European noblemen toured the West in style, with servants to hand them their guns and champagne to drink after the hunt. Railroads began to feature special excursion

KANSAS STATE HISTORICAL SOCIETY.

Shooting Bison from a Union Pacific Train. Walter Lockhart, 1931.

trains through buffalo country. As the trains chugged along, passengers could poke their guns through the open windows and fire away at the grazing herds.

By the 1860s, Indian tribes found that the buffalo were disappearing from their traditional hunting grounds. When they went elsewhere to hunt, they were followed almost immediately by white hunters, soldiers, and settlers. "Wherever the whites are established, the buffalo is gone," complained the Sioux Chief White Cloud, "and the red hunters must die of hunger."

Indians who once had been friendly to white people vowed to go on the warpath. Alarmed by the large-scale slaughter of their herds, angry warriors from many tribes banded together. They began to attack wagon trains, ranch houses, and railroad construction crews.

There were still about eight million buffalo left on the plains in 1870, when a newly invented tanning process sealed the fate of the remaining herds. For the first time, commercial tanneries in the East could turn buffalo hides into expensive leather. A single hide now brought as much as $3—more than a factory worker earned in a week in those days. A professional hide hunter could bag as many as two hundred buffalo in one day.

Organized bands of hide hunters shot their way south from Kansas to Texas. Armed with powerful long-range rifles with telescopic sights, they began to slaughter buffalo at the rate of a million a year. As the animals fell, gangs of skinners stripped them of their valuable hides and left the carcasses to rot on the prairie.

Indian war parties attacked the hide hunters wherever they found them, but the hunters could not be stopped. Within a few years, the

Scavengers of the Plains. Drawing by Theo. R. Davis, from *Harpers Magazine*, February 24, 1872.

Indians saw their main source of food, clothing, and shelter vanish.

At one time, perhaps sixty or seventy million buffalo had roamed the plains. By the early 1880s, the endless herds had been wiped out. Only a few hundred wild buffalo were still hiding out in remote mountain valleys.

With the buffalo gone, the proud and independent Plains Indians became a conquered people. Their way of life was destroyed, their hunting grounds taken over by white ranchers and settlers. Swept by starvation and disease, the great hunting tribes were confined to reservations, where they depended on government food rations. Their children were sent to boarding schools to learn the language and customs of the white man.

LIBRARY OF CONGRESS.

The days of the buffalo hunters had faded like a dream. But Indian storytellers still gather on winter nights to keep the old tales alive. They speak of a time when buffalo ruled the plains, and Indian warriors rode out to meet them.

I go to kill the buffalo.
The Great Spirit sent the buffalo.
On hills, in plains and woods.
So give me my bow; give me my bow;
I go to kill the buffalo.

SIOUX SONG

The Herd on the Move. William J. Hays, 1862.

AMON CARTER MUSEUM, FORT WORTH.

About the Illustrations

Most of the illustrations in this book are reproductions of paintings and drawings by artist-adventurers who traveled west when Indians lived in tipis and depended on the buffalo.

George Catlin of Philadelphia made a series of journeys into unmapped Indian territory between 1830 and 1836, visiting most of the major tribes from the Upper Missouri River to the Mexican Territory in the far Southwest. Carrying his canvases, paints, and notebooks, he wandered alone from tribe to tribe, fearlessly entering Indian villages, where he was greeted with courtesy and friendship. At the time, only a few fur trappers and traders had penetrated the region. The outside world knew practically nothing about the people who lived in the wilderness beyond the Mississippi. "Catlin's Indian Gallery," as the artist himself called it, consisted of hundreds of paintings and drawings portraying scenes of Indian life.

Another pioneering painter of the American West was Karl Bodmer, a Swiss artist who accompanied his patron, Prince Maximilian of Wied, on a 2,500-mile journey up the Missouri from 1832 to 1834. They traveled through the territories of the Sioux, Mandan, Blackfoot, and other tribes, where Bodmer completed more than 350 paintings and sketches notable for their beauty and accuracy.

Working before the age of photography, Catlin and Bodmer were the first to provide a comprehensive picture of the Plains Indians. They were followed by other eyewitness artists who went west to record a vanishing way of life. By the time Albert Bierstadt painted his *Last of the Buffalo* in 1888, the buffalo were almost extinct and the Plains Indians were confined to government reservations.

Unit District #5 Elementary
Instructional Media Center -2

Traditional Indian artists also portrayed the buffalo and the chase, but their work represented a different vision. Unaffected by the white man's art, Indian artists developed a unique and vivid style of their own, producing paintings and drawings that were more abstract and symbolic than "realistic."

Indian painting wasn't meant to be framed and hung on a museum wall. It decorated buffalo robes and tipi walls, war shields and saddlebags, and all sorts of leather items that were used, worn out, and replaced. Most of this art has long since rotted or disappeared. Only a few traditional Indian paintings depicting buffalo and buffalo hunts have survived.

Index

(Italicized numbers indicate pages with photos)